For the storytellers and artists. And for Jacob, who makes my favorite comics. — TNT

For all my Black woman cartoonist friends and peers. We are a beacon of light, innovation, and change. — SW

Text copyright © 2023 by Traci N. Todd
Illustrations copyright © 2023 by Shannon Wright

All rights reserved. Published by Orchard Books, an imprint of Scholastic Inc., *Publishers since 1920.* ORCHARD BOOKS and design are registered trademarks of Watts Publishing Group, Ltd., used under license. SCHOLASTIC and associated logos are trademarks and/or registered trademarks of Scholastic Inc.

The publisher does not have any control over and does not assume any responsibility for author or third-party websites or their content.

No part of this publication may be reproduced, stored in a retrieval system, or transmitted in any form or by any means, electronic, mechanical, photocopying, recording, or otherwise, without written permission of the publisher. For information regarding permission, write to Scholastic Inc., Attention: Permissions Department, 557 Broadway, New York, NY 10012.

Library of Congress Cataloging-in-Publication Data available

ISBN 978-1-338-30590-6

10 9 8 7 6 5 4 3 2 1   23 24 25 26 27

Printed in China   38
First edition, January 2023

The text type was set in Bernhard Gothic Medium. The display type was set in Corvinus Skyline. The illustrations were created digitally, using Adobe Photoshop CC. The book was printed on 140 gsm Golden Sun woodfree paper and bound by RR Donnelley Asia Printing Solutions Limited. Production was overseen by Lisa Broderick. Manufacturing was supervised by Shannon Rice. The book was art directed by David Saylor, designed by Shannon Wright and Charles Kreloff, and edited by Cassandra Pelham Fulton and Kait Feldmann.

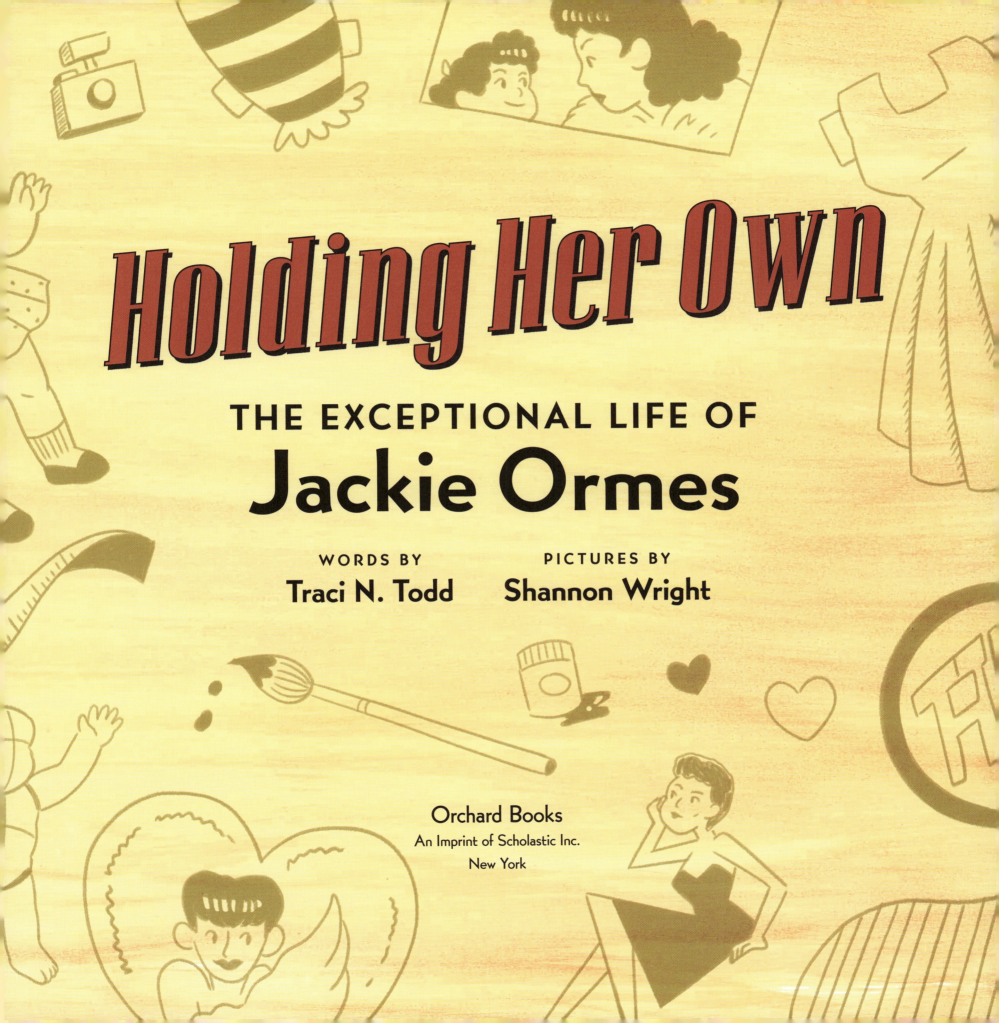

Holding Her Own

THE EXCEPTIONAL LIFE OF
Jackie Ormes

WORDS BY
Traci N. Todd

PICTURES BY
Shannon Wright

Orchard Books
An Imprint of Scholastic Inc.
New York

This story begins — as many stories do — with a blank page, an empty space waiting to be filled . . .

Zelda Jackson is an artist.
Her mother shows her how to work a needle and thread.
Her father owns a print shop and has a talent for painting.

Her big sister likes to sing, but mostly, she hides the soap so Zelda can't carve it into funny little beasts.

And Zelda fills every space she can find.

As she grows, Zelda becomes a poet and a storyteller, stitching together pictures and words. Yearbook pages filled with her funny drawings and snappy notes are a favorite at Monongahela High. And her happy rhymes about life at school tell the truth.

Zelda dreams of writing for the *Pittsburgh Courier*, the powerful Black newspaper published in the big city not too far away. When she writes to the editor asking for a job, her words are clever and quick, bobbing and weaving from one thought to the next. The editor asks for another letter, then another, and at last he asks:

FIGHT NIGHT!

Zelda sits in the second row, steps away from the other sports reporters and close enough to hear the

WHOMP! of each punch,

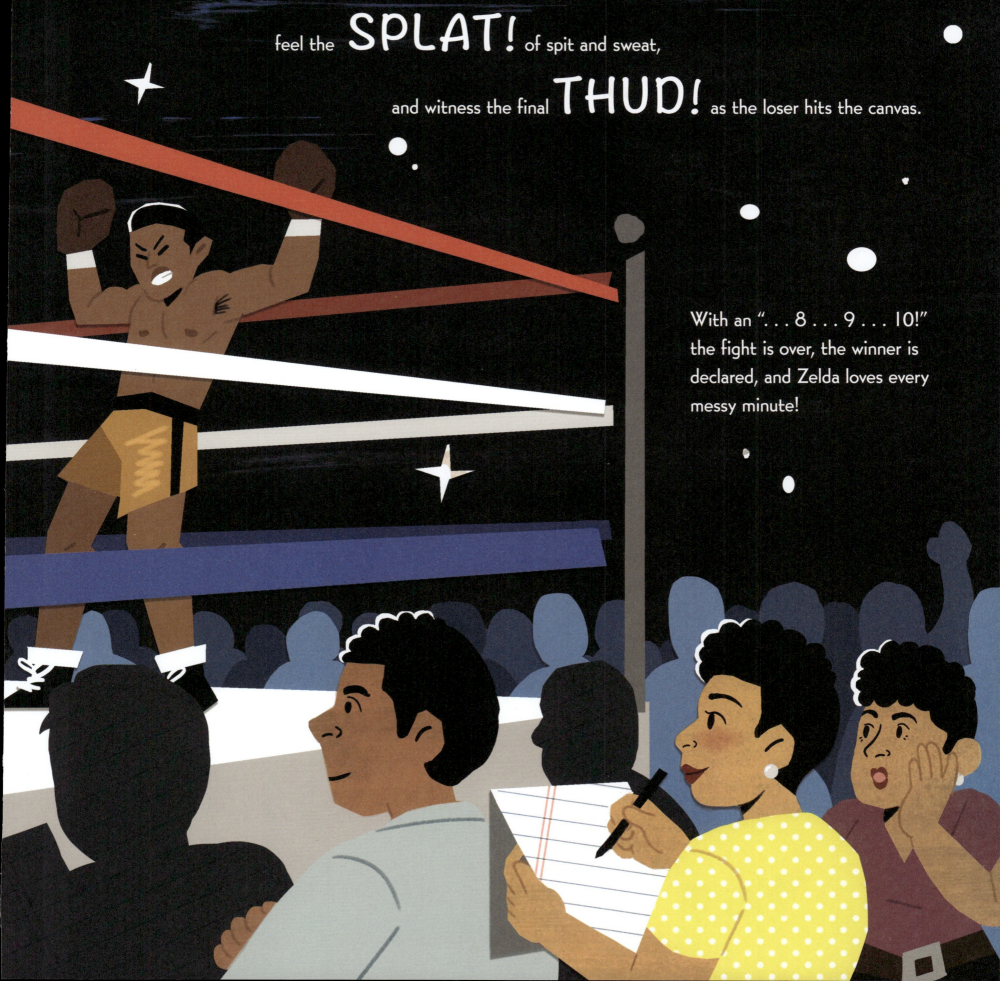

feel the SPLAT! of spit and sweat, and witness the final THUD! as the loser hits the canvas.

With an "...8...9...10!" the fight is over, the winner is declared, and Zelda loves every messy minute!

Zelda races home and writes down every last detail — from the colors the fighters wore, to the tiny typewriter held by one of the other sports reporters.

Then — Hello, Public! There's her story! On the "women's activities" page, not the sports page with the rest of the sports news. And her byline is simply her family nickname: "Jackie."

She pushes her way onto the *Courier*'s funny pages with a comic strip about Torchy Brown, who dreams of fame and fortune in New York, far away from her Mississippi home. Jackie gets the idea from stories she reads in the *Courier* about Black people fleeing southern towns for the hope and promise of northern cities. And she's inspired by the jump and jive of Harlem.

There is music in these panels, and not just from the characters who sing onstage. It's in the rhythm of Jackie's line, and in the quiet, mighty ways her characters confront prejudice and fear.

But it'll never last.

Well, what do they know? Torchy is a hit! But after just one year, Jackie puts down her pen to have a few adventures of her own.

The Sutherland Hotel is not known for welcoming Black customers, but with Earl as manager, the doors open wide. There's a barbershop and a beauty parlor where guests can get ready for a fancy night in the jazz lounge.

Louis Armstrong comes to play (and stay). Duke Ellington leads the band, and Sarah Vaughn shulie-a-bops 'til she can't shulie-a-bop no more! The Sutherland is the hottest spot in town!

But not everyone's life is so perfumed and fine.

There is trouble in the streets of Chicago. It's the same old trouble Black folks face everywhere — heightened by the Second World War. The promise of wartime jobs brought new waves of Black people to Chicago from the South. Men who joined the navy trained at a naval base just outside the city. And when the base allowed Black and white sailors to train together for the first time, Jackie reported the story for the *Chicago Defender*.

People who came to join the war effort, but not the war, had to push into the already-crowded blocks of Chicago's Black neighborhoods. And they pushed into workplaces where they were not wanted.

Now the war is over, the jobs are gone, and Black folks are still fighting — not just in Chicago, but all over the United States. Fighting for the promise. And Black women are on the front lines.

Some lift their voices on picket lines.
Some teach.
Some link arms and march.
Jackie is a fighter, but she isn't much for marching. So she finds another way.

Jackie sits before a blank page.

How can I be honest and true with enough Jackie joy?

She draws a few strokes of hair, a rounded cheek.
A stout belly and short, chubby legs.
The perfect dress, some shiny shoes . . . and here is the answer:

H'LO!

I'M PATTY-JO

Everything about Patty-Jo, from what she says to what she wears, is meant to make people smile. Because when times are hard, a little joy can feel like hope.

That hope spreads from coast to coast, in all fourteen editions of the *Courier*, touching more than a million people a week.

Jackie knows that sometimes money can feel like hope, too. She uses her fame to throw fantastic parties and fashion shows, raising money for all the causes that matter to her.

Over in Washington, DC, people in power are afraid. Afraid of the very change that Jackie and others are fighting for. Afraid because they cannot imagine that this change is necessary and good. Because they cannot imagine an America big and broad enough to truly welcome everyone.

So the people in power send spies to watch Jackie. They fill page after page with nervous notes about where she goes and who she sees.

But they never look at her comics. If they had, they'd have found proof of Jackie's big, broad imagination. And they would have seen Patty-Jo looking back, boldly poking fun.

Oh, that Patty-Jo. She really is a doll, isn't she? *Shouldn't she be?*
　　Jackie makes a pattern, cuts it into cloth, and stitches together a funny little thing. Then she tries molding clay until those round cheeks and chubby legs are just right.

At last, she teams with a toy company to make a Patty-Jo doll.
Jackie paints her lips, eyes, and signature brows by hand.
Jackie has always loved dolls, and there is none like Patty-Jo.

After twelve years, Jackie writes and draws her last Patty-Jo comic. For a little while, she draws Torchy again, too. But Torchy's time has come and gone.

The funny papers have changed, and Jackie is tired.
She tries one last time to get something started at another paper, but they want her to be part of a comics-making team.

Jackie Ormes is an artist.
Her mother showed her how to work a needle and thread.
Her father owned a print shop and had a talent for painting.

Now Jackie spends her days painting, too.
Mostly the faces of children.
None of them is Patty-Jo.

At last, when Jackie's hands no longer listen, and the ideas no longer flow . . . she puts down her brushes and leaves the next page . . .

"I always like to see the cheerier side of everything and everybody."

— Jackie Ormes

A NOTE FROM THE AUTHOR

This book would not have been possible without the foundational work of Nancy Goldstein. I'm grateful for her time and resources. I am also grateful to Skyla S. Hearn, archivist and special collections librarian at the DuSable Museum of African American History, and G'Jordan Williams, archives associate, for their help with Jackie Ormes's personal papers.

Jackie Ormes (named Zelda Jackson at birth) was born in 1911 just outside of Pittsburgh, Pennsylvania. She lived with her parents and older sister, Delores. Jackie's father owned a print shop and an outdoor movie theater. There are some accounts that he was also an artist, possibly a painter, but this is up for debate. At the very least, he had an eye for layout and poster design, and it's possible that Jackie inherited some of her artistic talent from him. Jackie's mother encouraged her children to be creative and musical, and she taught them how to sew.

When Jackie was six, her father died. Her mother remarried and the family moved to Monongahela, Pennsylvania, where life felt comfortable and safe. Jackie and Delores were anxious to see what the rest of the world was like, but for the time being, they would just have to imagine.

Jackie's imagination made her a gifted writer and poet, and her way with words landed her a job as a columnist for the *Pittsburgh Courier* while still in high school. The *Pittsburgh Courier* was once the most widely read Black newspaper in the United States. Founded in 1907 by a security guard and writer named Edwin Harleston, the newspaper rose to prominence when Robert Lee Vann took over in 1910, the year before Jackie was born. It was Robert who hired Jackie to join the paper's staff. The *Pittsburgh Courier*, *Chicago Defender*, and other Black-owned newspapers around the country amplified the voices and concerns of Black people when their voices went unheard in the white press. The newspapers also helped create a sense of pride and community.

Jackie liked chasing stories, especially because she was often given access to information her male coworkers were not, but Jackie *really* wanted to draw. Inspired by *Courier* articles about Black people leaving hard, dangerous lives in the South for the promise of safety and greater opportunities in the North, Jackie created a comic strip called *Torchy Brown in "Dixie to Harlem."* In the comic, Torchy leaves her Mississippi farm life, hoping to become a famous singer in New York. *Dixie to Harlem* debuted in the *Courier* in 1937, making Torchy the first Black woman to star in a newspaper comic. And because the Torchy strip ran in all of the *Courier*'s editions from coast to coast, Jackie was the first nationally syndicated Black woman cartoonist.

In 1942, Jackie moved to Chicago with her new husband, Earl Ormes. They settled in Bronzeville, a neighborhood on the city's South Side. It was home to the majority of Chicago's Black population and Black-run businesses. Jackie wrote for the *Chicago Defender* and studied at the Art Institute of Chicago. Earl worked in insurance and hotel management, and in the 1950s, he became the manager of the Sutherland Hotel. Prior to his arrival, the Sutherland did not welcome Black patrons, but by 1952, it was one of the few hotels in Chicago that was open to both Black and white guests. Many Black celebrities stayed at the hotel when they were in town, and some became Earl and Jackie's good friends.

While at the *Defender*, Jackie started a comic strip called *Candy* about a wisecracking housekeeper. When *Candy* ended after only a few months, Jackie was ready for something new. She pitched an idea to her old friends at the *Courier*: a strip about a spunky little girl and her beautiful, silent sister. *Patty-Jo 'n' Ginger* debuted on September 1, 1945, the same year World War II ended.

Jackie used *Patty-Jo 'n' Ginger* to comment on Black life, the war and its aftermath, and the fight for social justice. Many Black soldiers signed up to fight thinking that if they showed their loyalty to the United States, they would no longer be discriminated against. The war also created many manufacturing jobs in cities like Chicago, and Black people once again came from the South looking for work. But there were laws in Chicago that said Black people could only live in certain parts of the city, and with the arrival of new workers, housing in those areas became extremely crowded and unsafe. Black men fought hard for jobs that were only available to white men. Black women fought even harder. They faced discrimination because of their race *and* their gender.

When the war ended, the manufacturing jobs went away, and new jobs were hard to find. Banks wouldn't loan Black people the money they needed to afford nicer homes, and families who could afford to move were often terrorized if they tried to move outside of the city's Black neighborhoods. The push against these forces, in Chicago and other cities across the country, gave rise to the modern civil rights movement.

"Me, I was always fighting battles. I was anti-everything-that's-smelly."

— Jackie Ormes

Patty-Jo 'n' Ginger brought Jackie a considerable amount of fame, and she moved in influential circles. She used her stardom to support causes she believed in, like better housing and better schools for Black communities all over the country. She did as much as she could to help the poor and the struggling, and that caught the attention of the Federal Bureau of Investigation (FBI).

Beginning in the late 1940s, under the leadership of J. Edgar Hoover, the FBI watched organizations and activists like Jackie who sought justice and empowerment for the less powerful members of

American society. Hoover called these activists "subversives" and "radicals" and saw them as a threat to the "American way" of life.

The FBI spied on Jackie for ten years. They interviewed her several times, talked to her friends, and assembled a file with 287 pages of evidence of "troublesome" behavior. But there was nothing in Jackie's FBI file about her comics.

Jackie continued to draw *Patty-Jo 'n' Ginger*, and soon created a Patty-Jo doll. She partnered with the Terri Lee Doll Company, known for its Terri Lee doll. The Terri Lee company used one mold to make its dolls, so they all had the same body. But the dolls' faces were painted by hand. Jackie worked with the Terri Lee company to find the right shade of brown paint for Patty-Jo's skin, and taught the doll factory artists how to paint Patty-Jo's distinctive mouth, eyes, and brows. She even painted some of the dolls' faces herself.

"What'cha mean it's no game for girls? We got feet too, ain't we?"

"It would be interestin' to discover WHICH committee decided it was un-American to be COLORED!"

When it came to Patty-Jo's wardrobe, there was no question that she would have the finest, most fashionable doll clothes imaginable. Jackie also wanted children to be able to wash, brush, and curl Patty-Jo's hair. The Patty-Jo doll debuted in 1947 and was available for two years. The doll was marketed to Black families, but only those who made a comfortable living could afford it.

In 1950, Jackie brought Torchy back once more, this time in full color in *Torchy in Heartbeats*. Torchy was still an adventurer, but she also became a hero for environmental causes and racial justice. While *Torchy in Heartbeats* was Jackie's last new comic, it ran in the *Courier* until 1954. *Patty-Jo 'n' Ginger* ran until 1956.

Jackie lived in Chicago until her death in 1985.

A NOTE FROM THE ARTIST

As a Black woman cartoonist, I've been familiar with Jackie Ormes's work for some time, but I hadn't truly delved into her life and work until I was asked to illustrate *Holding Her Own*. When reading Traci's script, I found that her words reflected the wit, humor, and wise insights that were very much present in Jackie's own writing and comics. While creating the artwork for this book, I fell in love with Jackie Ormes and all she did as a spearhead for creators like me.

Illustrating this book was an extra-special experience, but it was also difficult for many reasons. Being in this profession, there are times when I feel the isolation and all-encompassing loneliness of working in a white-dominated industry as not only a Black artist, but as a Black woman. I sometimes find myself being silenced by peers, pressured to conform to impossible standards, and encouraged to let go of parts of myself to make people around me feel comfortable, to be more palatable: all challenges Jackie faced in the midst of a government afraid of the visibility and power that Black Americans were beginning to harness. Afraid of the power and light that she and so many others had to share.

The beauty this story brings is to be celebrated because, while it does come with its fair share of heartaches and obstacles, so much joy and happiness sprang from Jackie's hands and touched people's lives in her day, and that joy can still be felt now. I was able to weave parts of myself into each page of this book, and I included parts of history from Jackie's life in the walls of a scene, the floorboards of a spread, and even the fabric of a well-crafted dress. I poured bits and pieces of myself into the page with paint strokes from my brushes, found patterns, and misshapen scraps of paper. As an artist, I celebrate a woman who opened a door for me that might not have otherwise existed — a door that I plan to keep open as the next generation makes their way through it.

SELECTED BIBLIOGRAPHY

Books

Drake, St. Claire, and Horace R. Cayton. *Black Metropolis: A Study of Negro Life in a Northern City*. Chicago: University of Chicago Press, 1970.

Goldstein, Nancy. *Jackie Ormes: The First African American Woman Cartoonist*. Ann Arbor: The University of Michigan Press, 2008.

Whaley, Deborah Elizabeth. *Black Women in Sequence: Re-inking Comics, Graphic Novels, and Anime*. Seattle: University of Washington Press, 2015.

Newspaper Articles

Jackson, David. "The Amazing Adventures of Jackie Ormes." *Reader*, August 16, 1985.

Jackson, Zelda "Jackie." "Hello, Public." *The Pittsburgh Courier*, October 12, 1929.

Ottley, Roy. "Southside Hotel Meets Change." *Chicago Tribune*, April 15, 1956.

The Pittsburgh Courier, "Torchy Brown Will Be Big Hit in the Courier." August 12, 1950.

Personal Papers

Jackie Ormes Papers, Box 27fol20020190322. Hamilton Institute for Research and Civic Involvement, DuSable Museum of African American History, Chicago, IL.

CREDITS

Photos and art ©: 12 center: From *Jackie Ormes: The First African American Woman Cartoonist* by Nancy Goldstein, © 2008 University of Michigan Press; 21 skirt: *Torchy Brown in "Dixie to Harlem"* art by Jackie Ormes, from The Ohio State University Billy Ireland Cartoon Library & Museum; 34-35 background: Doll pattern art by Jackie Ormes, from the DuSable Museum of African American History; 36: *Torchy in Heartbeats* art by Jackie Ormes from the *New Pittsburgh Courier* and The Ohio State University Billy Ireland Cartoon Library & Museum; 42, 43: From *Jackie Ormes: The First African American Woman Cartoonist* by Nancy Goldstein, © 2008 University of Michigan Press; 44 top and bottom: published with permission from *Pittsburgh Courier* archives. All newspaper article and map images are from the *New Pittsburgh Courier*.